Souvenir and W

Cron ....

Louise Maskill

The Hill, Cromford

CURLEW
PRESS

Published by Curlew Press
Derbyshire

Email: mail@curlewpress.co.uk

All rights reserved. No part of this publication may be reproduced, stored in a retrieval system or transmitted in any form or by any means, electronic, mechanical, photocopying, recording or otherwise without the prior permission of Curlew Press.

British Library Cataloguing in Publication Data: a catalogue record for this book is available from the British Library.

1st Edition

ISBN: 978-1-9161044-2-6

Print – Gomer Press, Llandysul, Ceredigion SA44 4JL

Text – Louise Maskill

Walks – Karl Barton and Mark Titterton

Proofreader – Ian Howe

Design and layout – Mark Titterton

Photographs – Karl Barton – p.63 bottom Mark Titterton – p.9 top, p.13, p.15, p.21 bottom, p.24, p.27, p.34 bottom, p.35, p.36, p.38, p.38, p.39, p.42, p.43 all, p.44 all, p.46, p.47, p.48, p.50, p.51 top left & right, p.52 all, p.53, p.56 all, p.57, p.61, p.63 top Ben Tynegate - Cromford Mills – p.34 top right

Archive Photographs – Glynn Waite Collection - p.1, p.6, p.7, p.10 both, p.12 all, p.14, p.16 left, p.17, p.18 all, p.19, p.20, p.21 top, p.22, p.23 all, p.25 all, p.28 bottom, p.31 bottom, p.32, p.60 Courtesy of Lindsey Porter – p.28 top Ken Askew – p.33 both Arkwright Society – 34 top left and 51 bottom Buxton Museum and Art Gallery – p.5 Peak District Mining Museum – p.4, p.59 Paul Deakin – p.9 bottom Picturethepast.org.uk – p.16 right

Maps – © OpenStreetMap Contributors (openstreetmap.org)

Cover – Scarthin, Cromford

Contents

Souvenir and Walker's Guide to Cromford

Introduction and Early History

The village of Cromford is situated some 17 miles north of Derby in the rocky Derwent Valley, carved by the fast-flowing River Derwent through the soft Derbyshire limestone. The earliest record of the village is a scattered farming hamlet with around ten households mentioned in the Domesday Book of 1086, functioning as a supporting settlement to the larger town of Wirksworth some two miles to the south.

The village remained within the parish of Wirksworth, and by 1750 it had grown to around ninety dwellings. Despite its proximity to Cromford, Scarthin was in many ways a separate settlement, following the course of Bonsall Brook and extending through the Market Place and up the hillside towards Harp Edge. It was part of Matlock parish, although the two communities were intertwined and interdependent.

In the mid-eighteenth century the inhabitants were mainly lead miners and their families; there was also some quarrying and farming activity, although most of the pasturage was described as inferior, being hilly and rough and disturbed by lead mining. All the important local families (the Gells, Evans, Nightingales and Hurts) made money from mining, smelting and trading in lead, an industry which was carried out in accordance with the local barmote laws.

An engraving of Cromford titled 'A view in Crumford near Matlock Bath Derbyshire', c.1776

View at Cromford, Derbyshire, taken from the bridge, by William Day (1764–1807). The smelting mills (left) were demolished in the mid-1790s to make way for the building of St Mary's Church.

There was at least one medieval corn mill in Cromford, on the site now occupied by Arkwright's mill yard; this was demolished by Arkwright to make room for his second mill, but it was recorded from the thirteenth century. Lead smelting mills were also built by the river, resulting in water rights being in high demand to power bellows, mill wheels and other early industrial equipment.

Sir Richard Arkwright and the Industrial Revolution

The most dramatic period in the history of Cromford began in 1771, when Sir Richard Arkwright arrived. In association with his partners, Samuel Need and Jedediah Strutt, he leased a small area of riverside land with the intention of building an experimental water-powered cotton mill.

Water was critical in Arkwright's choice of Cromford as the location for his experiments. The River Derwent is a major outflow for rainwater deposited further north in the Peak District; its relatively constant and fast flow means that it was superbly suited to industrial uses. Cromford's other natural watercourse is the Bonsall Brook. It is now culverted beneath the village before it joins the Derwent, but it once powered at least thirteen industrial sites along its course. Over the centuries the Derwent and its tributaries have powered corn mills, sawmills, colour works, stone mills, smelters, calamine mills, paper mills and textile mills.

However, Arkwright's industrial advances in Cromford were made possible by the presence of drainage soughs, the first of which was built by Cornelius Vermuyden in the seventeenth century to drain the lead mines of the Wirksworth ore field. The extensive and branching Cromford Sough, built in many stages from the mid-seventeenth to late-eighteenth centuries, was an excellent choice to power a mill because the flow was strong and almost constant throughout the year, and because the water came from so deep underground that it rarely froze.

Arkwright's first experimental water-powered mill stood five storeys tall and eleven bays long, and was powered by Cromford Sough. His second mill was built in 1776–7, partly funded by Peter Nightingale, when a deal between the two men allowed Arkwright to demolish the medieval corn mill and facilitated access to development land and properties in the village. The second mill had seven storeys and was built hard against Scarthin Rock, blocking the road to Matlock Bath (which was diverted across the bridge that still survives in the mill yard).

A third mill, Masson, was constructed in 1783; this was the only mill which was driven directly by the Derwent. Masson Weir was built across the Derwent probably at the same time; its construction is unusual in that it curves downstream, perhaps in an attempt to tame the notoriously tempestuous river.

An early twentieth-century photograph of Arkwright's original mill (1771) taken from Mill Road

Opposite page: The waterwheel at the original mill

CROMFORD. THE WHEEL. ARKWRIGHTS OLD MILL.

The first mill was extended in 1785 with the addition of four bays so that it straddled Bonsall Brook as well as the sough, and at that time Arkwright also made a series of improvements to the other watercourses in the village. Greyhound Pond was created, and the Bear Pit, a short, exposed section of Cromford Sough, was excavated to allow the addition of a sluice gate to control the flow and fill the pond. This caused later problems for the mines upstream; water in the sough backed up against Arkwright's sluice and parts of the sough allegedly collapsed. Several mines were flooded, and Arkwright was taken to court by the mine owners and required to pay for repairs to the sough, as well as a yearly rent of £20 for the use of the water.

Arkwright quickly exhausted the supply of labour from the local area, and by 1781 he was starting to adopt a family employment model, attracting whole families to move to Cromford by offering purpose-built accommodation, mill work for the women and children, and framework knitting and handloom-weaving employment for the men, who were not required in the mills in such numbers. Some skilled men were brought in to build and maintain the mill machinery, and others were trained as clerks, accountants, joiners, mechanics, stonemasons and engineers.

A working day in the mill was thirteen hours long, but this included paid mealtimes (a half-hour for breakfast, an hour for dinner) when family members would bring food and heat it on stoves in the dinner-room. Arkwright's employees received free medical assistance, and sick workers (including children) received half-pay, with holidays on Christmas Day, Good Friday, Shrove Tuesday, Whit Monday and the local wakes. The Arkwrights were viewed as lenient employers; Manchester millworkers could expect to work much longer days with shorter breaks, fewer holidays and no sick pay for children.

Estimates from 1802 suggest that the size of the village had doubled since Arkwright's arrival thirty years earlier, with the mills employing 1150 people, of whom 700 were children. In 1816 Richard Arkwright Junior attested to a government enquiry that no children under ten had worked in the Cromford mills during the preceding decade, although prior to that children as young as seven had been taken on. Of 725 people employed in the mills at that time, 269 were under eighteen.

Opposite top: The Bear Pit **Bottom:** Cromford Sough

Above: Masson Mill **Below:** Another view of Arkwright's mill from the bottom of The Hill

This view of The Tors shows the cut through Scarthin Rock. The building on the left was one of the lodges belonging to Willersley Castle.

Transport Links

Prior to the Industrial Revolution, travel in rural Derbyshire had always been challenging. Some roads leading to and from Cromford were improved when rich landowners constructed private routes for their own use, but the public were still restricted to more difficult ways over high ground until the Turnpike Acts of the early eighteenth century created more reliable routes. The road from Cromford to Bonsall following the Bonsall Brook was one of these; the old road linking the two settlements had gone over the hillside.

Arkwright himself improved the turnpike from Cromford to Matlock Bath; originally the route had passed over the imposing Scarthin Rock via a natural depression, but it must have been steep and difficult to traverse. Arkwright blasted through the rock around 1777, and the route was further improved around 1818 when the turnpike from Cromford to Belper (the current A6) was opened. However, the cut through Scarthin Rock remained narrow, originally just wide enough for a single coach. The road was improved to its current width in the 1960s.

Top and above: The Wharf, Cromford Canal

Leawood Pump House

Water routes were also vitally important for industrial transport. Cromford Canal was engineered by William Jessop and Benjamin Outram, opening in 1794 and linking the Cromford mills with the wider canal network and later the Cromford and High Peak Railway. The canal was fed by water outflow from the mills, with a massive Boulton and Watt beam engine, built in 1849 at Leawood Pump House, lifting additional water from the Derwent when necessary.

Cromford Wharf was built on land that was originally part of the estate of Rock House, Arkwright's family residence, and for many years the Arkwright family kept a pleasure boat on the canal, housed in the boat house which can still be seen on the far side of the wharf basin. The Cromford Canal Company was operated by the local Wheatcroft family, who went on to become successful

Leawood Pump House from the aqueduct on the Cromford Canal

boat owners and hauliers down several generations and across many sites in the Midlands. The canal carried heavy traffic for many decades, but the railways eventually took over and Cromford Canal finally closed in 1944.

The final link in the freight transport network, the Cromford and High Peak Railway, opened in 1831, joining Cromford Canal to the Peak Forest Canal at Whaley Bridge. It negotiated a series of inclines linked by level stretches; wagons were pulled up the inclines by stationary engines, and drawn along the level stretches initially by horses and later by locomotives. The Wheatcrofts utilised the railway for freight, and tourists could even take a ride on the C&HPR; the line was briefly licensed to carry passengers, although they had to walk up and down the inclines, and the service was discontinued after a fatal accident in 1877. The line finally closed in 1967 after a gradual but terminal decline in traffic.

Above and opposite: Cromford Station

Passenger rail traffic came to Cromford in 1849 with the opening of a line between Ambergate and Rowsley operated by the Midland Railway, one of the two main backers. The original plan was to build a station at the southern end of Cromford Meadows, but failure to agree the details with the landowner resulted in a small temporary station with wooden buildings being erected in the cutting at the mouth of Willersley Tunnel. This became the permanent location in 1850. Stone-built structures and platform extensions were subsequently added to provide much of the scene we see today.

The station master's house and structures on both the upside (Derby-bound) and downside (Matlock-bound) lines were built between 1855 and 1875. The footbridge was built in 1885 to facilitate passenger access between the two platforms, when increasing traffic made the previous boarded level crossing undesirable.

In 1963 Cromford Station was among many identified for closure in the infamous Beeching Report, but it was saved in 1967, although Sunday services were withdrawn. The line from Ambergate to Matlock was singled in 1969 with the upside line track being lifted; this meant that the platform and waiting room on that side of the station were no longer required. However, the footbridge was retained to provide access to the station master's house; both this and the former waiting room are now in private ownership. The building on the downside was converted into a Scout hostel in the 1970s, but later fell into disrepair. It was renovated by the Arkwright Society between 2007 and 2009 and converted into two office suites.

Other Local Industries

Lead mining and quarrying had been the most significant local industries before Arkwright's arrival, and they continued to be important in the local economy. Lead mining in particular provided employment for whole families, with men and boys extracting ore while women and children processed it for smelting. Mining was governed by the strict local barmote laws, which gave miners the right to prospect for lead on any land that was not a public highway, a garden or a churchyard.

The industry went into decline locally and nationally after the late eighteenth century because of worked-out veins and increasing extraction costs, but evidence of mining activity can still be seen in the local landscape; fields are pocked with the evidence of small-scale mining activity, and the hills are riddled with the tunnels, caverns and drainage soughs left by larger workings.

The calamine (zinc ore) industry was not governed by the same strict rules as lead mining, but the ore extraction process was similar and smelting houses could be converted. Brassmakers from Birmingham had interests in

Gentlemen outside the offices of the local hauler company N. Wheatcroft & Son

Workmen at Dene Quarry in the 1950s

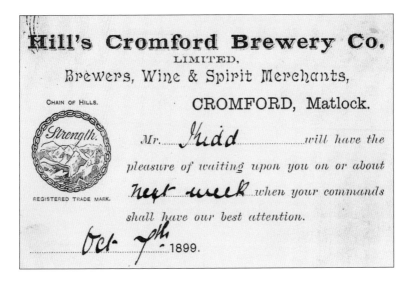

the Cromford area, leasing land to build calamine mills; there are reports of up to 400 tons of calamine being produced annually in Cromford in the early years of the nineteenth century, and a mill in the centre of the village continued to process ore into the 1820s.

Brewing was associated with various pubs in the village, as well as with buildings in the mill complex after they were vacated by the Arkwright family. Matthew Hill in particular began a brewing business at the Greyhound in 1876, and by 1890 the operation was housed in the Barracks building on the mill site.

The Troy Laundry occupied surviving buildings from the second mill from 1895. The laundry was established to serve the growing hotel trade in Matlock and Matlock Bath, using water from Bonsall Brook after filtration and purification. It did considerable business, especially during the Second World War when the military shipped in laundry from bases as far afield as Lincolnshire. It declined during the 1950s with the growth of household washing machines, finally closing in 1966.

The Via Gellia Colour Company, later the Cromford Colour Company, leased and then purchased mill buildings from 1914 onwards, producing chrome-based colours for use in paints and printing inks, for the domestic and export markets. Pigments were mixed and pressed into hard, dry cakes, which could then be stored and ground down into powders to fill customer orders.

Rock House, Arkwright's family home

Notable Families

Arkwright brought his family to Cromford in 1776, taking a lease on Rock House overlooking the mills, and they remained at the centre of village life for the next 150 years. Arkwright acquired the manor of Cromford in 1789, and he and his descendants were squires until Frederick Arkwright died in 1923.

Arkwright bought the manor from Peter Nightingale, a landowner and industrialist who lived at Woodend, on the way to Lea. Nightingale was Arkwright's financier, but he also built his own mill at Lea in 1783 in association with his partner, John Smedley. Today, Lea Mills is a unique survival of an original Arkwright-style mill on a site which

Woodend

is still involved in textile production. Now known as Smedley's, the operation continues to produce high-quality designer knitwear for clients as illustrious as Queen Elizabeth II.

Peter Nightingale was a great-uncle of Florence Nightingale, the pioneer of nursing reform. Florence was born in Italy in 1820, but her father William had inherited Lea Hurst in Lea, and the family came to live there on their return from Italy. Florence loved Lea Hurst; after her return from the Crimea she lived mostly in London, but returned to Derbyshire regularly, often arriving by train and alighting at Whatstandwell to walk up to her family home.

George Evans was also significant in the industrial transformation of Bonsall and Cromford. He was a banker and financier who lived in Cromford Bridge House, and owned a succession of industrial sites along Bonsall Brook, including corn mills, lead smelters and a calamine mill. One of his smelters was at the Via Gellia site at the foot of the Clatterway; the site later housed a textile mill and was acquired by William Hollins, who developed Viyella (a fabric woven from merino and cotton) in the late nineteenth century. Although the fabric was never manufactured at the Via Gellia site, the name Viyella was derived from the name of the mill where it was invented.

Another local industrialist, Jedediah Strutt, was a co-signatory on Arkwright's lease of the first mill site in 1771, and also built his own mills in Belper and Milford, south along the Derwent, from 1776 onwards.

Cromford Bridge House

Buildings and Landmarks

Arkwright moved into Rock House, overlooking his mills, in 1776. The original building probably dated from the mid-eighteenth century, but it has been extensively remodelled, not least by the Arkwrights themselves over several generations. The house was converted into flats in 1933 and has remained in private ownership ever since.

In 1786 Arkwright commissioned Willersley Castle on the other side of the river, intending this to be his family seat. The house was built with local stone, and was designed to resemble a castle with pleasure gardens, a gatehouse, hothouses and a walled kitchen garden. Construction did not run smoothly; the builders had to excavate down to the bedrock before they could construct the piers for the house, and a fire in 1891 destroyed much of the internal work.

Arkwright died at Rock House in 1792 before Willersley was complete, leaving direction in his will that his son, also Richard, should finish the house as well as the chapel by Cromford Bridge. The younger Richard and his family moved into Willersley four years later, and the estate stayed in the Arkwright family until 1923 when the house became a Methodist Guild holiday centre. Today it is a hotel run by the Christian Guild, open all year for coffee, lunch and afternoon tea.

Scarthin and Greyhound Pond

Opposite page: Willersley Castle

The Greyhound Hotel, Cromford Market Place

In the village itself, the most imposing building is the Greyhound Hotel, formerly the Black Greyhound or the Black Dog, built on the Market Place during Arkwright's rearrangement of the village in 1778–9. Next to it is the Shambles, a single-storey row of shops, originally permanent market stalls and still in use today. This is the last surviving trace of the regular Saturday market which was held here from 1790.

Greyhound Pond, behind the hotel, stored water for the mills and was probably created during Arkwright's 1785 rearrangement of the Cromford watercourses. A sluice in the corner nearest the Boat Inn controlled the flow to an underground culvert, which runs under the Market Place and on to the mills.

On The Hill, the Cromford Institute was funded by Frederick Arkwright in 1897–8 to celebrate Queen Victoria's Diamond Jubilee. The Institute provided a home for the St Mark's Men's Institute, and once housed a billiard room and a reading room. It is still well used as a community space today.

North Street comprises facing terraces of three-storey gritstone cottages built by Arkwright to attract workers for his second mill. The houses have well-lit upper floors to facilitate framework knitting and handloom weaving work. Each house had a garden plot and luxurious architectural details such as sash windows; they would have been extremely desirable workers' residences.

Cromford Primary School, at the end of North Street, was built by Richard Arkwright Junior in 1832 in anticipation of the 1833 Factories

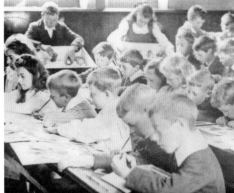

Top left: A shopkeeper outside the Shambles **Right:** A class at Cromford Primary School
Above: North Street

Act, which mandated employers to combine mill work with education for children older than nine (and also made it illegal to employ children younger than this). Arkwright's mill children split their days between education and factory work, a pattern known as half-time schooling. Mill children did not pay for their education; others were welcome to attend if their families could afford the weekly fee of tuppence.

Cromford Bridge was built in the fifteenth century, and the original medieval pointed arches can be seen on the downstream side. It was later widened, and has more modern rounded arches on the upstream side. The small building by the bridge was once a cottage, converted from farm

Cromford bridge chapel

buildings by Richard Arkwright Junior; its current use as a fishing lodge is in imitation of the more famous lodge on the River Dove used by Izaak Walton, author of *The Compleat Angler*. The Cromford version is still used by the local angling club – the inscription above the door, 'piscatoribus sacrum', means 'sacred to fishermen'. Next to the lodge are the ruins of a medieval bridge chapel, taken down by Richard Arkwright Junior in 1797 and turned into a 'picturesque ruin' to enhance the elegance of the views from Willersley.

Pubs and Churches

St Mary's Church stands by Cromford Bridge, originally a chapel commissioned by Arkwright when WIllersley Castle was also under construction. Like Willersley, however, it was not completed until after his death. It had been planned as a private chapel, but when it was consecrated in 1797 it was agreed that it should be a public place of worship for Cromford residents, the parish church in Wirksworth being two miles distant. In 1869 it became Cromford Parish Church.

St Mary's was remodelled over many decades, notably by the removal of the original gallery and the addition of wall paintings by Alfred Hemming and stained glass to celebrate the church's centenary in 1897. In 1978 dry rot was found in the roof, necessitating a twenty-year closure and an extensive programme of repairs funded by the diocese, the Arkwright

St Mark's Chapel

Society and the local community. The church is now recognised for its architectural and historical importance.

St Mark's Chapel was built when Cromford Parish separated from Wirksworth Parish in 1869, and was consecrated in 1877. It was built on open land on The Hill and was originally intended as a mortuary chapel with a burial ground, since the parish did not have a churchyard for public use. However, it was soon in use for services of all kinds, except marriage for which it was not licensed. It was demolished in 1970 after dry rot forced closure in 1963, although the churchyard remained in use until 1992; the lychgate survives on St Marks Close.

In contrast to the manorial land of Cromford, Scarthin was not estate-owned, and one difference between the two settlements is the number of Nonconformist places of worship in Scarthin. All but one are now converted to other uses, but the village was once home to Wesleyan Methodists, Wesleyan Reformers, Primitive Methodists and General Baptists. The Wesleyans opened the first chapel in 1808, near the foot of Chapel Hill which is named after it. The Primitive Methodists opened

Wesleyan Chapel on Water Lane

a chapel at the top of Scarthin in 1854, while the Reformers built their chapel around 1862 on the hillside above what is now Scarthin Books.

The various flavours of Methodism eventually united in 1932 and met at the Mount Tabor Chapel, which had been extended from the Reformers' chapel in 1907; the frontage is still clearly identifiable next door to Scarthin Books. Mount Tabor closed in 1958 and the congregation moved to the Wesleyan Chapel on Water Lane, the only Nonconformist place of worship in Scarthin still in use. The Anglican Church opened a Mission Chapel in 1869, also on Water Lane; the building is easily recognisable as a former church, although it now houses a garage. The Anglican and Nonconformist congregations in Cromford and Scarthin regularly united to contribute to local celebrations, with Friendly Societies and combined church choirs and bands marching together during the many galas and parades that were staged by the two communities.

The local pubs must also have contributed greatly to these events; indeed, it is said that Arkwright encouraged his workers to drink beer rather than the local water, since the latter was likely to be contaminated by lead. The Greyhound on the Market Place was built by Arkwright to provide accommodation, luncheons and teas for businessmen, investors and the growing tourist trade; it also once contained a branch of Lloyds Bank. Close by, on Scarthin, the Boat backs onto Greyhound Pond and is still a pub. It used to be known as the Hit or Miss, with the name changing to the Boat in the mid-nineteenth century because the landlord at that time used to be a boatman on the canal. The operation once included a brewery in the adjoining buildings.

Meanwhile, the Cock Inn and the Bell Inn stood opposite each other on the corners of North Street. The Bell, on the uphill corner of North Street, was formerly the Blue Bell, and is one of the few brick-built buildings in Cromford. It is known to have been a licensed premises since 1828, and is still trading as a pub. The Cock ceased to trade as a public house around 1897 and became a tea room offering refreshments to tourists; it also had function rooms where religious and community societies met. The building bears a plaque with the date '1730'; it is now in residential use.

Many other buildings in Cromford once operated as public houses. The Crown was at the bottom end of The Hill and was trading in 1842; this building still exists, although it is now a private residence. Similarly, a private house about halfway up The Hill was once the Red Lion, while a residence at the corner of Steeple Grange and Oakerthorpe Road (at the top of The Hill, on the way to Wirksworth) used to operate as the Railway Inn.

St Mary's Church

Above: The Railway Inn

Right: The former Cock Inn on the corner of North Street, operating here as the Tea Rooms

Other pub buildings are now long gone. The George and Dragon was located near Cromford Bridge, while the Bull's Head and the Wheatsheaf were on Scarthin; all of these buildings are now lost, along with the King's Head (which once stood by the side of Masson Mill), the Rutland Arms (in a terraced row opposite Masson Mill) and the Junction Inn (at Lea Mills).

Of course, all these pubs were counterbalanced during the nineteenth century by a local Temperance Society urging moderation in alcohol consumption; Cromford's Temperance Hall once stood on Scarthin, close to the Primitive Methodist Chapel and overlooking Greyhound Pond. It was recorded as old and derelict in 1893, but it was renovated in that year by Frederick Arkwright and presented to the residents of Scarthin in the 1920s. It was used for dances, suppers and other community events, and the Scouts met there. It was demolished in the 1950s or 1960s during a period when many of the old terraced houses in Scarthin were also levelled.

Cromford after the Arkwrights

By the 1830s employment in the mills was starting to decline. The Arkwrights were reluctant to invest in modernisation, but the end of the family's active investment in Cromford came in 1839, when Richard Arkwright Junior lost his legal battle against the proprietors of Meersbrook Sough, which drained water from the Wirksworth lead mines at a lower level than Cromford Sough. This reduced the Cromford flow to a point where the mills could no longer function profitably.

During the nineteenth century the textile industry migrated northward to Lancashire and Cheshire, and Cromford was limited in its recovery and expansion potential by its geographical position and relative inaccessibility. However, the Arkwrights entered partnerships to keep Masson Mill in business; by the late nineteenth century Masson was the only Cromford mill making any profit, spinning yarn for the new domestic sewing machine market. It continued in operation until 1922.

The Cromford mill buildings were gradually leased out for alternative uses: corn storage, laundry, brewing, warehousing, smaller-scale textiles, paint production, and even a trout farm. The second mill burned down in 1890, and the top two storeys of the first mill were also lost to fire in 1929 when the building was in use as a colour works. Other buildings also burned down, notably the Barracks which had once provided accommodation for unmarried men who worked at the mill.

The Arkwrights' involvement with Cromford finally ended with an estate sale in 1924, after the last squire, Frederick Arkwright, died in 1923. The estate was sold off by his heir to meet ruinous death duties; tenants in the estate cottages, which included most of the village, were given the opportunity to buy their homes at nominal prices. Willersley Castle and the Cromford Mills complex were put up for sale in 1927, Masson having been sold in 1897.

There was also a general loss of employment in the wider area due to the decline of the lead mining industry, and between the wars Cromford entered a period of economic decay, with limited employment opportunities and a population decline as young people moved away to find work. The village missed the Arkwrights' financial support as well, with the school, the churches and other community organisations all suffering.

The major success story was limestone quarrying, with a number of large-scale operations commencing at this time. Ball Eye, Slinter Top and Dene Quarries opened or reopened during these years, drastically altering the shape of the village; Dene Quarry in particular has caused the loss of farms, roads and houses from a hillside area of just over 170 acres.

Artists and Writers

Alison Uttley, née Alice Taylor, was born 1884 at Castle Top Farm on the hillside above Lea Road. She was a gifted scientist, becoming only the second woman to graduate from Manchester University with a degree in Physics, and she went on to become a science teacher in London. She took up writing to support herself and her son after her husband's suicide in 1930; her best-known books are the *Little Grey Rabbit* series, but she also wrote *The Country Child*, a fictionalised account of her childhood at Castle Top Farm, and *A Traveller in Time*, which is based on the Babington Plot to free Mary, Queen of Scots from nearby Wingfield Manor. The Babington family lived at Dethick, near Cromford.

The painter George Turner was born in Cromford, the son of Thomas Turner, a tailor and draper, and his wife Elizabeth. George was a talented artist from a young age and may have been self-taught; he came to be known as 'Derbyshire's Constable', working in oils and creating idyllic pastoral scenes inspired by the lush fertile landscape of southern Derbyshire, where he later settled with his first wife Eliza and their four children. After Eliza's death, however, George moved back to the Cromford area, remarrying and settling in Kirk Ireton and later moving to Idridgehay, where he died. He is buried in Idridgehay churchyard.

DH Lawrence grew up at Eastwood, near Nottingham, but he and his wife Frieda lived at Mountain Cottage overlooking the Via Gellia for just under a year in 1918/19. While they were there he wrote a short story set in the local area, *Wintry Peacock*, and he must have known Cromford well; he later used it to inspire the village of Papplewick in *The Virgin and the Gypsy*, and Cromford Station was used as a location in a film adaptation of the book in 1970.

Local Tales and Traditions

There is an inscribed stone on Cromford Bridge, bearing the words 'The Leap of BH Mare June 1697'. This is believed to relate to a Mr Benjamin Hayward of nearby Cromford Bridge House (later owned by the industrialist George Evans), whose horse was travelling at too great a speed to make the sharp turn onto the bridge. Horse and rider overshot, leaping the low stone parapet and plunging into the Derwent some ten feet below, but miraculously both are said to have survived the incident, the horse landing in the water and swimming to shore with Mr Hayward still in his saddle.

Inscribed stone on the parapet of Cromford Bridge

Arkwright introduced festivals and holidays to the local calendar. The annual celebratory tradition of 'candlelighting' began at his mill in Nottingham, and in September 1776 it coincided with the opening of his second mill on the Cromford site. There was a 500-strong procession around the village headed by a band and a boy on a cart engaged on a loom, culminating in food and ale at the mill and an evening of music, dancing and singing.

When Arkwright introduced candlelighting there was no public place of worship in the village, but when St Mary's Chapel was consecrated the

Floats and decorated bicycles on the Market Place, perhaps celebrating the coronation of King George V and Queen Mary in June 1911

ceremony merged with the traditional wakes celebration. Wakes were once a national religious observance, with every community celebrating the festival of the parish church's patron saint; in Cromford this falls on the nearest Sunday after 8 September, the Nativity of the Virgin Mary. During the Industrial Revolution these religious festivals evolved into week-long secular events when the workforce would take their annual holidays while mills and factories were closed for maintenance.

Cromford and Scarthin had the local reputation of 'going to town' to celebrate the local wakes as well as national occasions such as jubilees, coronations or victories in war. Wakes Week in Cromford involved open-air worship, a carnival, processions, dancing, music recitals and other community events, raising money by collection for local good causes and being very well attended by the community. Bunting was hung in profusion, church bells rang, and cannon were fired from Willersley. Illuminated boats were floated on Greyhound Pond, and the streets were decorated with arches, flowers and signs celebrating the event. Schoolchildren were usually given the week off school for the celebrations; this practice continued well into the twentieth century, ending only in 1936 when school holidays were standardised across the country.

Bustum and Bunkum's Circus, was this a float in the carnival?

Cromford Carnival, 1934

Left: Restoration of the Cromford Mills, c.1970s   **Above and below:** Cromford Mills today

Cromford Today

By 1843, after two generations of Arkwrights had turned the village on its head, Cromford was scarcely recognisable as the scattered lead mining and farming community where Sir Richard had arrived in 1771. However, the subsequent years of economic decline also left their mark, with buildings standing derelict and the population shrinking as lack of employment forced relocation.

The restoration and preservation of the village's industrial heritage was triggered by the highly successful Arkwright Festival in 1971, celebrating 200 years since the great man's arrival. The festival's organisation committee evolved into a permanent body, the Arkwright Society, which has since been well supported locally, nationally and internationally. It funded the purchase of most of the mill site in 1979, with the remainder being acquired in 1988; this has been a massive restoration project, but the surviving industrial heritage is now being carefully preserved.

Due largely to the Arkwright Society's efforts, the Derwent Valley Mills (an area stretching from Masson Mill in the north to Derby Silk Mill some 15 miles downriver to the south) was granted UNESCO World Heritage status in 2001. The Derwent Valley's geographical inaccessibility meant that the urbanisation of mill towns such as Manchester during the nineteenth and early twentieth centuries never reached Cromford, which contributed to the survival of this unique cultural landscape in the birthplace of the Industrial Revolution.

Cromford Mills is now run as a heritage attraction, with shops, galleries, tours, walks, events, cafés and a Visitor Centre. Masson Mill houses a shopping centre and museum, while Cromford Wharf and Canal have also undergone a major restoration of the waterway and industrial buildings. The canal is now plied by Birdswood, a historic canal boat offering scheduled trips and private charters, and the waterway is an important wildlife conservation site; it is owned and managed by Derbyshire County Council as an SSSI, with a recent resurgence of the elusive water vole.

The Cromford and High Peak Railway is also preserved; the locomotives are long gone, but starting at High Peak Junction the trackbed now forms the High Peak Trail, providing some 17 miles of accessible walking and cycling through the beautiful Peak District. It is joined by the Tissington Trail at Parsley Hay, and also forms part of both the Pennine Bridleway and the Midshires Way. (Please see the Bibliography for some excellent walking books taking in the High Peak and Tissington Trails – also published by Curlew Press.)

In the village itself there are shops, places to eat and drink, tourist accommodation, and of course the renowned Scarthin Books, the self-styled 'bookshop for the majority of minorities'. Cromford is well worth a visit, both for its fascinating industrial heritage and for its vibrant community spirit which has come down the generations since the days of the lead miners and mill workers.

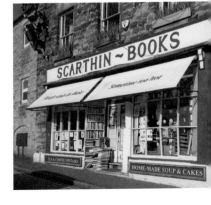

The Walks

About the Walks

The walks in this guide all start from the Market Place in Cromford (postcode DE4 3QE).

These walks are suitable for the reasonably fit, ranging in distance between two and five miles. The routes will take you across fields and through woodland as well as along roadside pavements; sturdy walking boots and appropriate clothing are essential. For further details please see the essential information for each walk.

Weather conditions can be checked online at www.metoffice.gov.uk. While the maps in this guide are accurate, they are intended to be used in conjunction with a detailed Ordnance Survey map, such as the OS Explorer OL24 (1:25 000 scale) covering the White Peak area.

Getting There

Public Transport

Train: Services are currently run by East Midlands Railway.

Table 56 of the national rail timetable details an hourly service between Matlock and Nottingham from Monday to Saturday and a two-hourly service on Sunday. In reality the majority of services run to and from Newark Castle.

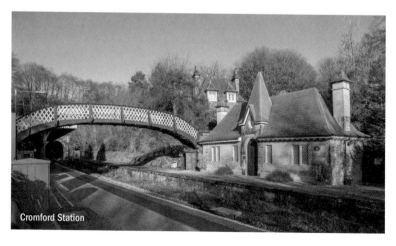

Cromford Station

Cromford Station lies three quarters of a mile from Cromford Market Place, the starting point of all these walks. However, the walk to Lea Bridge passes Cromford Station and the Matlock Bath walk passes within 200 yards of Matlock Bath station.

www.nationalrail.co.uk

www.eastmidlandsrailway.co.uk

Bus: Cromford is well served by buses, to a variety of destinations. The following stop either at or within 100 yards of Cromford Market Place.

Operator	Route	Principal stops
Trent Barton	6.1	Bakewell – Matlock – Wirksworth – Belper – Derby
Hulleys	110/111	Matlock – Wirksworth – Ashbourne
Littles	140	Matlock – Crich – Alfreton
Littles	141	Matlock – Crich – Ripley
High Peak	Transpeak	Derby – Belper – Matlock – Bakewell – Buxton

www.travelineeastmidlands.co.uk

www.highpeakbuses.com

www.hulleys-of-baslow.co.uk

www.littlestravel.co.uk

www.trentbarton.co.uk

By Car: Cromford is located just off the A6 south of Matlock at the bottom of The Hill (B5036). From the motorway exit the M1 at junction 28 and take the A38 towards Derby and take the A610 towards Ambergate and Matlock. At Ambergate head north on the A6 towards Matlock for about five miles to arrive at Cromford.

Parking: Off-road parking is available on the Market Place and adjacent to the Memorial Gardens at the bottom of The Hill (honesty box). There is limited roadside parking on Water Street and The Hill; check restrictions when parking. The nearest alternative is at Cromford Wharf (2 Mill Road, Cromford DE4 3RQ) pay and display car park.

1. Cromford Village Walk

Essential Information

Facilities: Pubs include the Greyhound Hotel on the Market Place, the Boat Inn on Scarthin and the Bell Inn at the end of North Street on The Hill. There are numerous cafés and options for takeaway food in the village. Toilets with disabled facilities are located at the bottom of The Hill in the Memorial Gardens (fee charged).

Distance and Approximate Walking Time: 2 miles / 45 mins – 1 hour

Path Description: Roadside pavements and footpaths around the village.

About the Walk

This walk is a short but fascinating amble around the villages of Cromford and Scarthin, taking you past many of the places mentioned in the earlier text. You will pass Scarthin Books (well worth a visit!), a number of chapels, old industrial sites, millworkers' cottages, inns, the school, the Bear Pit and the old village lock-up, finishing back in the Market Place with its many opportunities for refreshment.

Former millworkers' cottages on North Street

Pigsties near the Bear Pit

Directions

1. From the Market Place, take Scarthin behind the Shambles, passing the Boat Inn, the Post Office, the old Mount Tabor chapel and Scarthin Books, with views over Greyhound Pond to your left.

2. Opposite the Primitive Methodist Chapel, turn right onto a path and climb as it rises around the houses, following it for around 300 yards until you reach a T-junction with a broad track.

3. Turn left down the track to Chapel Hill. Close to the junction with Water Lane you will see the old Wesleyan Methodist Chapel on your left. At the junction with the main road, walk on a few yards to a point where it is safer to cross, and make your way to the pavement opposite. Over the wall is Cromford's second corn mill with its mill pond and dam, constructed by George Evans in 1780; the remains of a further mill and wheel pit are behind the current building. A gap in the stone wall leads to a little bridge spanning the sluice where water from the dam flows into a culvert underground to the waterwheel on Water Lane.
As you continue along Water Lane towards the Market Place you will pass the old Anglican Mission Chapel (now a garage), the former calamine and paint works with waterwheel still extant but not in use, the Methodist Church, and views towards Scarthin across Greyhound Pond to your left.

4. At the T-junction with the Greyhound Hotel on your left, turn right up The Hill, passing the Cromford Institute on your right.

5. Turn right into Alabaster Lane with The Old Cottage on your right. Continue along the road as it becomes a footpath.

6. At a staggered crossing of the path, turn left and cross Hawthorn Drive to take the path almost opposite.

7. Follow the path alongside the cemetery. To your right, at the top of the steps is the location of St Mark's Chapel, which succumbed to rot and was demolished in 1970.

8. At the foot of the steps, turn left down St Marks Close and then right following the road back to The Hill.

9. Turn left down The Hill.

10. Cross this busy road with care, and after a few yards turn right into North Street. With The Bell on your right, the building on the opposite corner was formerly the Cock Inn. Walk to the end of this beautifully preserved street, with its Grade II listed buildings. You will be returning here later in the walk for a second opportunity to take in the detail.

11. At the end of North Street is Cromford Primary School. Turn right between the trough and the last house on the street, following the path around the back of the houses. After the Old Cottage, bear left up a lane to bring you back out on The Hill. Turn left up The Hill.

12. After a few yards, take the first left along Bedehouse Lane. Follow Bedehouse Lane to the right as it becomes a path and ascends the hill. Skirt the left-hand side of the Bedehouses (almshouses), continuing uphill to the junction with Barnwell Lane.

13. Turn right into Barnwell Lane, walk to the end and turn right again onto The Hill. This is a busy road, but the walk back down to North Street gives you the opportunity to view the many millworkers' houses that line the road.

14. Turn right into North Street and follow it to the end once again.

15. At the end of the street, follow the road around to the left. Prior to the road passing between two stone gateposts, there is a gap in the wall on the left, close to a mature tree. Take the path beyond, following it to The Hill.

Along this path are several stone pigsties, the Bear Pit and Swift's Opening, a yard which once contained the village lock-up (now an art gallery).

16. Turn right back onto The Hill and return to the Market Place.

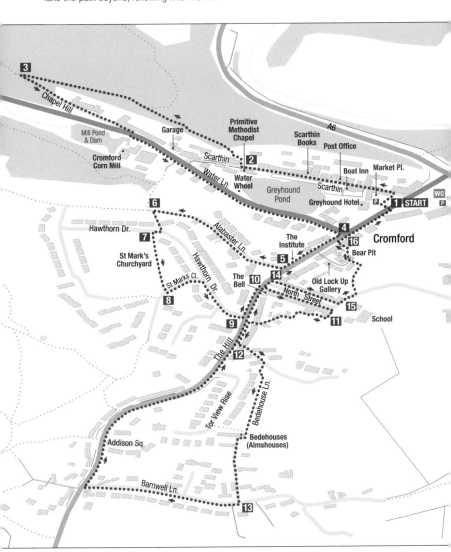

2. Matlock Bath Walk

Essential Information

Facilities: There are numerous options for food and drink in Cromford and Matlock Bath. Toilets with disabled facilities are located at the bottom of The Hill in the Memorial Gardens (fee charged) and in Matlock Bath Memorial Gardens just off the walking route (fee charged).

Distance and Approximate Walking Time: 4 miles / 2½ hours

Path Description: This is a short but fairly strenuous walk on footpaths through woodland which can become muddy and slippery, especially after heavy rain. There are several steep descents (and ascents), occasionally on steps which require care to negotiate; as such, this walk may not be suitable for families with young children. You may avoid one steep climb up the side of the Derwent Valley by walking along the roadside pavement from Masson Mill (point 5) to the Grand Pavilion in Matlock Bath where you rejoin the route (point 13); however, this would make for a rather lengthy roadside walk.

About the Walk

This walk takes you over Scarthin Rock to Matlock Bath, once a fashionable spa and now a busy tourist spot with an atmosphere all its own. Your route takes you past Arkwright's Masson Mill, now a shopping village, as well as a number of Matlock Bath's more modern attractions, and includes a riverside meander through the Derwent Gardens, originally laid out for the gentry taking the waters. You will return to Cromford via hillside roads which give spectacular views over Matlock Bath and the cliffs on the opposite side of the gorge.

Right: Matlock Bath

Matlock Bath – the Little Switzerland of England

The history of Matlock Bath as a tourist destination began in 1698 when baths were opened to take advantage of the warm springs welling up from the hillside. They were widely thought to have health-giving properties, and by the nineteenth century Matlock Bath had become a fashionable and prosperous society spa. It enjoyed royal patronage – Princess (later Queen) Victoria visited in 1832 – and attracted other illustrious health-tourists such as Lord Byron, John Ruskin and Josiah Wedgwood.

The Grand Pavilion was built for the tourist trade in 1910, providing a venue for musical and theatrical entertainment. Today it is owned and run by a community-led charitable organisation, saved from demolition and once more a valued amenity. It also houses the Peak District Mining Museum. An Aquarium and Petrifying Well may be found on the other side of North Parade, in a building which still contains a bathing pool fed directly by the thermal springs – although these days the only bathers are golden carp.

Today Matlock Bath has an atmosphere all its own – something of the seaside prom, with its amusement arcades, fish-and-chip shops, autumn illuminations (a popular local festival) and gaudy charm. It is a Mecca for motorcyclists on a sunny Bank Holiday, and a diverting place to visit at any time of the year.

Directions

1. From the Market Place, take Scarthin behind the Shambles, passing the Boat Inn, the Post Office, an old chapel and Scarthin Books.

2. Turn right up the footpath opposite the Primitive Methodist Chapel which rises at the side of a private house. Follow the path uphill around the back of the houses until the first waymarked path on your right joins from above at an acute angle.

3. Turn back on yourself and follow the waymarked path uphill as it takes you into the Derwent Valley.

4. Just beyond Cromford Court (a large house with many chimneys), take the right-hand fork in the path, following the wall line as the path descends steeply to the A6 in the valley below.

5. With Masson Mill in front of you, turn left and walk for around 300 yards.

6. Just before you reach the Old School House (on the other side of the road), take the path rising on your left towards the New Bath Hotel. Stay on this path, which almost immediately doubles back on itself and then

Cromford Court

turns to the right before beginning a steep ascent. Follow the path uphill between the walls (do not deviate from the main path), turning to the right along the low wall line as the ascent becomes easier.

7. Follow the path as it turns to the left to ascend more steeply towards Clifton Cottage.

8. Turn right at the cottage and follow the partially surfaced track to Upperwood Road for around 300 yards.

9. Prior to a small parking area, take the path on your right, which descends steeply through the woods via numerous steps and slopes. Keep a look out for an adit (the entrance to a lead mine) to the right of a flight of steps.

Masson Mill

Heights of Abraham

Upperwood Road **19**

Holme Road **18**

Waterloo Road

Matlock Bath

16

Jubliee Bridge

River Derwent

17

WC

Upperwood Road

Fish Pond
13
11

Lead Mining Museum

Grand Pavilion

10

9

12

Temple Road

14

A6

Derwent Gardens

Gulliver's Kingdom

15

7

New Bath Hotel

Clifton Cottage
20 **8**

6

River Derwent

Masson Mill

Willersley Castle

21

4

5

Cromford Court

22

3

Via Gellia

Primitive Methodist Chapel

Scarthin Books

Post Office

Market Pl.

2

Scarthin

The Hill

WC

Cromford

Greyhound Pond

Boat Inn

Greyhound Hotel

1 START

P

P

Above: Jubilee Bridge spanning the River Derwent, Matlock Bath

10. Where a path joins across the bottom of some steps, turn right, descending yet more steps at the side of the Gulliver's Kingdom chair lift.

11. Emerging on the drive for Gulliver's Kingdom, follow it downhill to Temple Road.

12. Turn right onto Temple Road, then almost immediately take the path on your left down to the Fish Pond pub.

13. Cross the road at the pedestrian crossing and then turn right to walk in front of the Grand Pavilion, home to the Peak District Mining Museum and the Restoration Café.

14. Take the drive down the side of the Pavilion, with the bowling green on your right. Follow the path as it meanders through Derwent Gardens, with its grotto and thermal springs.

15. Cross the footbridge and turn left, following the path alongside the Derwent until you reach and cross Jubilee Bridge.

16. On North Parade there is a pedestrian refuge immediately on your left; cross here to reach the various shops and cafés. Turn right and continue along North Parade until just before Tucker's Fish and Chips about 25 yards prior to the traffic lights and pedestrian crossing.

17. Take the stepped path which rises steeply between the buildings to reach Holme Road. Note the path is not signposted and may be easily missed.

18. Turn left, following Holme Road to the point where Waterloo Road drops to your left and Upperwood Road continues to rise.

19. Follow Upperwood Road back to Clifton Cottage.

20. At the fingerpost, continue along the path, rather than dropping down into the Derwent Valley.

21. Adjacent to Cromford Court we rejoin the path on which we started our journey.

22. Remember to make a sharp left when descending to Scarthin, then turn left on the road which descends to the Market Place and your starting point.

3. Lea Bridge Walk

Essential Information

Facilities: Pubs in Cromford include the Greyhound Hotel on the Market Place, the Boat Inn on Scarthin and the Bell Inn at the end of North Street on The Hill. There is a café at Cromford Mills. Toilets with disabled facilities are located at the bottom of The Hill in the Memorial Gardens (fee charged), at Cromford Mills and on the Cromford Canal at the High Peak Junction Visitor Centre and Cromford Wharf car park (subject to opening times).

Distance and Approximate Walking Time: 5 miles / 2½ hours.
Short route 1½ miles / less than an hour

Path Description: Includes footpaths through woodland which may be muddy underfoot, a section along the canal towpath and some walking on roadside pavement.

About the Walk

This walk starts with a bird's-eye view of the village and mills, and then takes in the station (perhaps familiar from the cover artwork for the 1995 single "Some Might Say" by Oasis?) and the houses of George Evans and Peter Nightingale, both contemporaries and sometime partners of Arkwright. The factory shop at Lea Mills is well worth a visit if you have time, while on the return leg along the canal you will visit High Peak Junction and see some of the industrial engineering achievements which carried goods to and from Cromford.

Right: The High Peak Junction on the Cromford Canal

Directions

1. From the Market Place, walk down The Hill and cross at the traffic lights, and then cross the A6 at another pedestrian crossing and turn left towards Matlock.

2. Prior to the bus stop, turn right through the gates into Church Walk.

3. After 100 yards or so, take the path on your right towards Cromford Mills, then almost immediately right again to climb the steep path and steps up Scarthin Rock for views over the mills and Willersley Castle.

4. Descend from Scarthin Rock the way you came up, and then turn left and immediately right to continue along Church Walk. On your left is the former site of a lead smelting mill, which later became a calamine mill. St Mary's Church, commissioned by Sir Richard Arkwright in the late 1700s, stands to the left of the path before it meets Mill Road.

5. At the end of the path, turn left onto Mill Road. After a short distance on the other side of the road you will see the fishing lodge once occupied by Arkwright's water bailiffs, next to the remains of the medieval bridge

Cromford Canal

chapel. Cross the bridge with care (the pavement narrows here).

6. Follow Lea Road, crossing Willersley Lane to the station approach. The house between Willersley Lane and Lea Road is Cromford Bridge House, previously Senior Field House, once the residence of George Evans whose bank became part of what is now NatWest/RBS.

7. Turn left to the station. Those familiar with the works of Oasis will recognise Cromford Station from the single and EP cover of "Some Might Say". The southern portal of

the 764-yard Willersley Tunnel can be seen at the end of the platforms.

8. Return to Lea Road via the steps from the station approach. If you are following the short route, now is the time to turn back to your right to follow Lea Road then Mill Road to reach point 19 at the Canal Wharf. Otherwise, turn left to walk under the railway bridge.

9. Around 50 yards beyond the railway bridge, take the footpath on your left uphill. As you climb the footpath, the building through the trees to your right is Woodend, the former residence of Peter Nightingale,

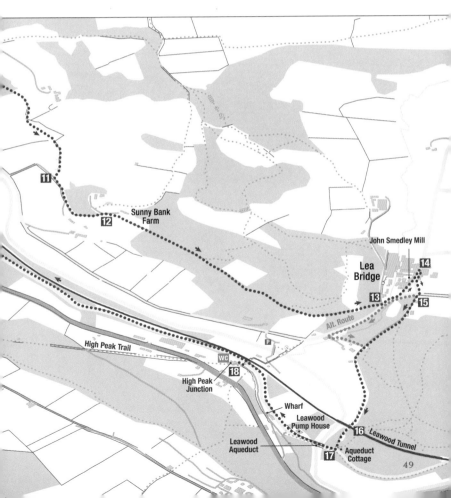

Lea Mills

who commissioned the house and moved there in 1795.

10. At a crossroads of paths, turn right and continue through the woods. Once in the open fields, after a short distance the path starts to descend, passing a couple of springs then after around another 250 yards the path joins a lane.

11. Turn left and follow the lane uphill as it skirts a wood.

12. As the lane makes a sharp deviation to the left, close to Sunny Bank Farm, take the path on your right, which takes you into Bow Wood. Follow the path as it descends to Lea Road at Lea Bridge.

13. Turn left up Lea Road for a look at the John Smedley mill, which is still in use for the production of textiles. Within the mill complex is the original mill, commissioned by Peter Nightingale and designed according to Arkwright's principles.

14. From the bridge connecting the factory buildings on either side of the road, turn around and take the left-hand road back to Mill Lane.

15. Almost opposite the road junction is a lane which takes you to the wharf on the Nightingale Arm of the Cromford Canal. If it is not possible to traverse the lane, return to Mill Lane/Lea Road and turn left, following the road to the bus stop and cottages where you can turn left and follow a footpath a short distance to the wharf, where you turn right.

16. Continue along the Nightingale Arm over the crossing of the former Midland Main Line, with the northern portal of Leawood Tunnel on your left. When you reach Cromford Canal you will see the Leawood Aqueduct on your right and the remains of Aqueduct Cottage on your left.

17. Turn right, following the tow path of the Cromford Canal (which opened in 1794) across the aqueduct towards Leawood Pump House. Further towards Cromford are the wharf buildings of the Cromford and High Peak Railway where goods could be transferred between canal and rail.

18. After taking a look around the exhibition at Cromford Goods, now known as High Peak Junction, continue along the towpath on the opposite side of the canal for a further mile to reach Cromford Wharf. Just before you

Cromford Canal

The Loom Shop, Cromford Mills

reach the wharf, on your left on the other side of the basin is the entrance to a tunnel, which led to Arkwright's boat house. Above the boat house you will see Rock House, the former residence of Richard Arkwright.

19. Take time to explore the wharf and its history, before leaving the complex and turning left into Mill Road.

20. Cross the road with care to reach the Grade I listed complex of Cromford Mills, a fascinating and well-preserved group of buildings and associated works which now forms the centrepiece of the Derwent Valley Mills UNESCO World Heritage Site.

21. After exploring the mill complex, turn right onto Mill Road. After a few yards you will notice an abutment on the other side of the road to the mill. This once carried a

Right: The former aqueduct destroyed in 2002

Grade I listed cast iron aqueduct that took water from Cromford Sough to feed an overshot waterwheel within the mill complex. The aqueduct was destroyed in November 2002 when a container lorry drove through it, and awaits restoration.

Continue along Mill Road, negotiating the pedestrian crossings over the A6 and The Hill to arrive back in Cromford Market Place.

Leawood Pump House

The Grade II* Leawood Pump House opened in 1849. The Boulton and Watt beam engine, which still steams on selected weekends throughout the year, is able to raise around four tons of water per stroke, lifting it from the Derwent via a 150-yard tunnel to a reservoir beneath the pump house.

4. Rose End Meadows Nature Reserve and High Peak Trail Walk

Essential Information

Facilities: Pubs include the Greyhound Hotel on the Market Place, the Boat Inn on Scarthin and the Bell Inn at the end of North Street on The Hill. There are numerous cafés and options for takeaway food in the village. Toilets with disabled facilities are located at the bottom of The Hill in the Memorial Gardens (fee charged).

Distance and Approximate Walking Time: 3 miles / 2 hours

Path Description: Footpaths and roadside pavement on the climb to the High Peak Trail.

About the Walk

Rose End Meadows nature reserve, which you will visit early in this walk, is a group of sixteen small fields which have never been treated with artificial fertiliser or pesticides, making them a very special survival of limestone farmland which is home to a wide variety of plant, bird and insect life. Your route also takes you along a section of the High Peak Trail with wonderful views of the village, and finally past the Bear Pit, the section of Cromford Sough that was exposed by Arkwright in order to insert a sluice gate.

View from the High Peak Trail

Directions

1. From the Market Place, carefully cross the busy Water Lane and head up The Hill towards Wirksworth.

2. Just beyond the Cromford Institute, take the first right into Alabaster Lane. Follow the lane to its end and keep going on the footpath. Stay on the main path, ignoring turns to the left and right. At the junction with the end of Rose End Avenue, continue ahead up the track, climbing a little more steeply as you go. Ignore a locked gate on your left and proceed a little further to another gate.

3. Turn left through the gate adjacent to a sign reading "Welcome to Rose End Meadows Nature Reserve". Note the warning signs alerting you to the dangers of capped mines; there are no fewer than 13 shafts in this section of the nature reserve alone. Follow the path across the fields, initially keeping the woodland to your right. Immediately after going through a gate the path meets a track, where you turn left. After a short distance there is a fenced-in dew pond on your left.

4. Exit the nature reserve through a gate and follow the path on the right to emerge back on The Hill.

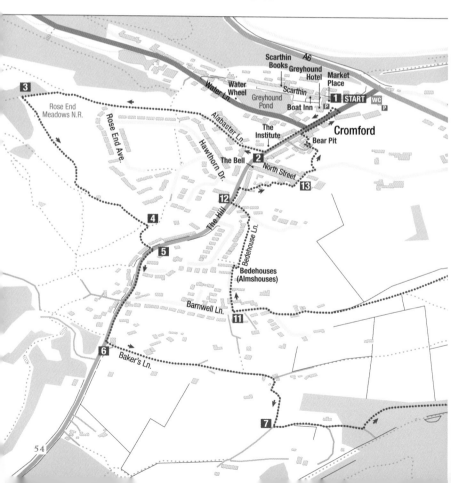

5. Cross the busy road with care and turn right, climbing The Hill. Cross three side roads, including a private road, until you reach Baker's Lane, which is just prior to the entrance to Dene Quarry over the road.

6. Turn left into Baker's Lane, with the premises of the Slinter Mining Company straddling the road. Follow it for around a quarter of a mile as it meanders steeply up towards Black Rocks.

7. Turn left towards Pineclouds, signed for the High Peak Trail. Continue into the woods, following the path to a stile in the stone wall

on the right at the edge of the woods. Cross the stile to reach the High Peak Trail.

8. Turn left on the trail. The views of Cromford and beyond to Matlock Bank are spectacular, with many of the features and places of interest noted in this book laid out before you. Reaching the engine house at Sheep Pasture Top, keep going to descend the incline.

9. Around quarter of a mile down the incline, adjacent to a quarry, a large fingerboard points to the right for Intake Lane. Follow this path down to Intake Lane and turn left,

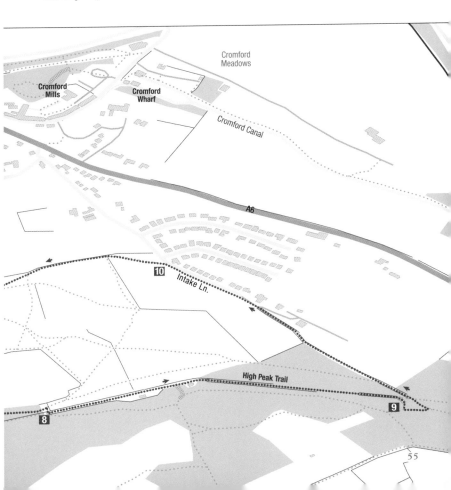

The Hill, Cromford

passing under the High Peak Trail. Continue down the lane, at first through the woods and then past houses, for a third of a mile.

10. At the end of a row of bungalows, as Intake Lane bends to the right, take the path on your left over the fields to Barnwell Lane, a distance of around a third of a mile. Turn right on the sealed road to stay on Barnwell Lane. The lane then bears sharply to the left.

11. Turn right down Bedehouse Lane, skirting the bedehouses (ancient almshouses once allotted to the deserving poor) and descending to The Hill.

12. Turn right down The Hill, and after a few yards turn right again on the public footpath to take you behind the houses of North Street.

13. Emerging at the end of North Street, continue with the school on your right, taking the path on your left through a gap in the wall to reach the stone posted gateway to Oakhill, now Alison House and The Vicarage. Follow the path as it passes the Bear Pit, emerging once again on The Hill. Turn right and return to your starting point in the Market Place.

Left: Remains of Sheep Pasture Engine House on the High Peak Trail

5. Slinter Wood and Via Gellia Walk

Essential Information

Facilities: Pubs include the Greyhound Hotel on the Market Place, the Boat Inn on Scarthin and the Bell Inn at the end of North Street on The Hill. There are numerous cafés and options for takeaway food in the village. Toilets with disabled facilities are located at the bottom of The Hill in the Memorial Gardens (fee charged).

Distance and Approximate Walking Time: 3 miles / 2 hours

Path Description: Some steep hills and steps with precipitous slopes close to the path edge. Paths may become muddy through Slinter Wood and over fields after periods of heavy rain.

About the Walk

This walk follows the course of the Bonsall Brook up the Via Gellia, passing mill sites along the way, before heading into woodland. (The Via Gellia supposedly got its mock-Latin name because the Gell family, of Hopton, claimed Roman ancestry – this may or may not be true!) The path takes you past quarry sites in Slinter Wood before heading back down into the village and passing the churchyard where St Mark's Chapel once stood.

Sluice, Bonsall Brook, Slinter Wood

Directions

1. From the Market Place, follow Scarthin to its end at the junction with Water Lane, crossing this busy road and taking the footpath almost opposite with Walkers Garage on your right.

2. Once beyond the stone stoops of the stile, take the path on your right into the woods, following it uphill to the base of a rock face. As you continue, glance through the trees below and to your right to see a mill pond and dam, which collects water from Bonsall Brook. The associated corn mill and attached cottage date to the 1780s.

A section of the path here follows a filled-in water channel or 'goit' which once ran to a second hillside corn mill (demolished

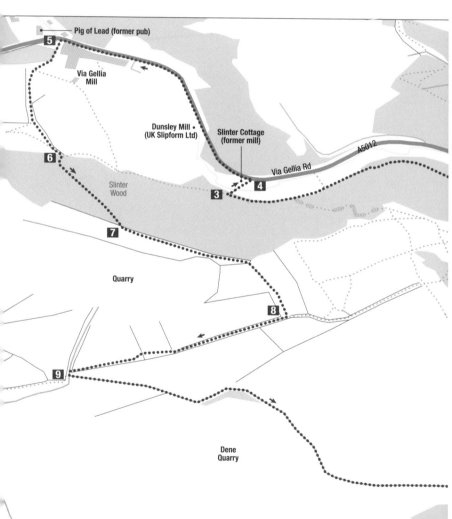

in the 1890s). Continue along the path which follows Bonsall Brook. You will pass a number of weirs, sluices, silted-up ponds and a boardwalk.

3. Cross the brook via a footbridge at the former sawmill, now Slinter Cottage. It was probably originally a smelting lead slag mill and later a bobbin mill for the Arkwright

estate, before becoming a sawmill in the nineteenth century.

4. Turn left on the pavement along the Via Gellia, passing the tall chimney of the former sawmill. As the road rises gently you will pass Dunsley Mill, formerly a paper mill, and Via Gellia Mill. Ahead of you over the road was the Pig of Lead public house, previously

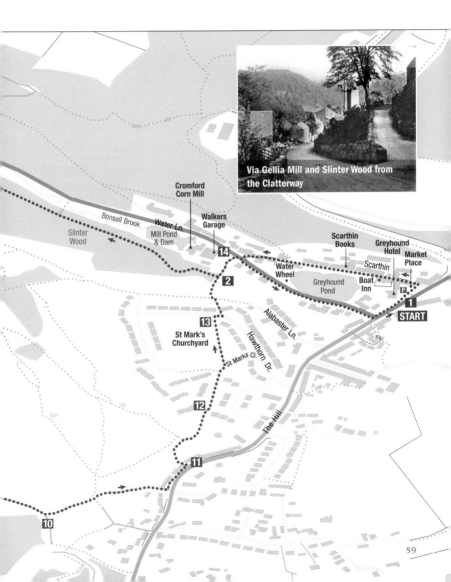

Via Gellia Mill and Slinter Wood from the Clatterway

the Via Gellia Inn and now offering bed-and-breakfast accommodation. The main Via Gellia road continues left up the valley towards Newhaven. The road to the right is the Clatterway and leads to Bonsall.

5. Turn left between the Mill Pond and Dunsley Mill, taking the steps up the hillside to a stile. Continue uphill through a field, and with the woodland in front of you, the path runs between two stone walls. Keeping the wall on your left, aim for the top-left corner of the field.

6. Go through the gate and immediately take the gate on your right to enter Slinter Wood. Ascend the hill, passing a gated adit near the top of the wood, to reach a stile in the stone wall, with its "Path Diverted by Legal Order" sign firmly affixed to a wooden post.

7. Immediately turn left and follow the waymarked path, with the pylons to your right and wall to the left. After a wooden gate, continue on the path across an open field to a junction of paths. There is an ornate metal garden gate on the path ahead.

8. Turn right here on the track (a continuation of Alabaster Lane), entering the avenue of trees. Continue along the path as it climbs to a stile onto a lane. Through

the trees on the left of the path old farm machinery sits atop a capped mineshaft.

9. Turn left and immediately left again down the limestone lane which descends around the edge of Dene Quarry. Follow this lane to the outskirts of Cromford.

10. About 50 yards short of the Dene Quarry yards, take the grassy track on your left. Stay on this path which descends to The Hill, where you turn left.

11. Between the houses numbered 86 and 84, turn left and follow the path to the right around the back of the houses, noting the stone steps on your left. Keep to the lower path with the wall line to your right.

12. The path emerges at the end of St Marks Close. Follow the road until you reach the lich gate to the former St Mark's Church. To the right of the lychgate is a small flight of steps, beyond which a path leads you to Hawthorn Drive.

13. Cross Hawthorn Drive and take the path opposite. Cross another path and head downhill to Water Lane.

14. Turn right and return to the Market Place, which is on your left at the end of Water Lane.

Above: Pig of Lead, Via Gellia   **Opposite page:** Slinter Cottage

Useful Information

Tourist Information Points

Ecclesbourne Valley Railway Ticket Office
Wirksworth Station, Station Road,
Wirksworth, DE4 4FB

High Peak Junction (on the Cromford Canal)
Tel: 01629 533105

Middleton Top (on the High Peak Trail)
Middleton by Wirksworth, DE4 4LS
Tel: 01629 533298

Peak District Mining Museum
Grand Pavilion, South Parade,
Matlock Bath, DE4 3NR

Peak Rail
Matlock Railway Station
Platform 1, Matlock, DE4 3NA
Tel: 01629 580381

Public Transport

See pages 36–7

Places to Visit

The Book Shop
Market Place, Wirksworth, DE4 4ET
Tel: 01629 825120

Birdswood
Weighbridge Office, Gothic Warehouse,
Mill Road, Cromford, DE4 3RQ
www.birdswood.org   Tel: 07552 055 455
Scheduled, horse-drawn and private charter
trips on the canal; see website for details.

Cromford Mills
Mill Lane, Cromford, Matlock,
Derbyshire, DE4 3RQ
www.cromfordmills.org.uk
Tel: 01629 823256

John Smedley Mill Shop
Lea Mills, Lea Bridge, Matlock DE4 5AG
www.johnsmedley.com   Tel: 01629 534160

Leawood Pump House
The nearest car park is for High Peak Junction,
Lea Road, Lea Bridge.
Leawood Pump House has regular steaming
dates throughout the year. Details can be found
on the Derbyshire County Council website.

Masson Mill
Derby Road, Matlock Bath, Matlock, DE4 3PY
www.massonmills.co.uk   Tel: 01629 581001
Working textile museum and shopping village.

Middleton Top Countryside Centre
On the High Peak Trail, Middleton by
Wirksworth, DE4 4LS   Tel: 01629 533298
Visitor centre and cycle hire. Middleton Top
Engine House is open to the public on certain
weekends throughout the year. Details can
be found on the Derbyshire County Council
website.

National Stone Centre
Porter Lane, Matlock, DE4 4LS
www.nationalstonecentre.org.uk
Tel: 01629 824833

Peak District Mining Museum
The Grand Pavilion, South Parade,
Matlock Bath, DE4 3NR
www.peakdistrictleadminingmuseum.co.uk
Tel: 01629 583834
The museum also offers guided tours to
Temple Mine just across the road.

Scarthin Books
The Promenade, Cromford, Matlock, DE4 3QF
www.scarthinbooks.com
Tel: 01629 823272
Book shop and café.

Wirksworth Heritage Centre
31 St John's Street, Wirksworth,
Matlock, DE4 4DS
www.wirksworthheritage.co.uk
Tel: 01629 707000